The Funniest KNOCK-KNOCK BOOK EVER!

Joseph Rosenbloom

illustrated by
Hans Wilhelm

Knock-knock.
  Who's there?
Eddie.
  Eddie who?
Eddie-body home?

Sterling Publishing Co., Inc.   New York
Blandford Press   Dorset, England

Knock-knock.
Who's there?
Anita.
Anita who?
Anita tell some knock-knock jokes.

Text copyright © 1986 by Joseph Rosenbloom
Illustrations copyright © 1986 by Hans Wilhelm, Inc.
Published by Sterling Publishing Co., Inc.
Two Park Avenue, New York, N.Y. 10016
Distributed in Canada by Oak Tree Press Ltd.
℅ Canadian Manda Group, P.O. Box 920, Station U
Toronto, Ontario, Canada M8Z 5P9
Distributed in the United Kingdom by Blandford Press
Link House, West Street, Poole, Dorset BH15 1LL, England
Distributed in Australia by Capricorn Ltd.
P.O. Box 665, Lane Cove, NSW 2066
Manufactured in the United States of America

Library of Congress Cataloging-in-Publication Data

Rosenbloom, Joseph.
  The funniest knock-knock book ever!

  Summary: An illustrated collection of over forty
knock-knock jokes.
  1. Knock-knock jokes. 2. Wit and humor, Juvenile.
[1. Knock-knock jokes. 2. Jokes] I. Wilhelm, Hans,
1945–   ill. II. Title.
PN6231.K55R66 1986   818'.5402   86-5989
ISBN 0-8069-4758-6
ISBN 0-8069-4759-4 (lib. bdg.)

Knock-knock.
   Who's there?
Wanda.
   Wanda who?
Wanda hear a knock-knock joke?

Knock-knock.
   Who's there?
Noah.
   Noah who?
Noah don't!

Knock-knock.
   Who's there?
Doris.
   Doris who?
Doris a puppy
in the window.

Knock-knock.
   Who's there?
Howard.
   Howard who?
Howard you like
to hold the puppy?

Knock-knock.
   Who's there?
Wooden shoe.
   Wooden shoe who?
Wooden shoe like a puppy, too?

Knock-knock.
   Who's there?
Olive.
   Olive who?
Olive the puppy.

Knock-knock.
  Who's there?
Luke.
  Luke who?
Luke out! There's a
hole in the boat!

Knock-knock.
  Who's there?
Rhoda.
  Rhoda who?
Rhoda boat across the lake.

Knock-knock.
  Who's there?
Otto.
  Otto who?
Otto know how to swim.

Knock-knock.
  Who's there?
Dwayne.
  Dwayne who?
Dwayne the lake—I'm dwowning!

Knock-knock.
  Who's there?
Jewel.
  Jewel who?
Jewel never
find me.

Knock-knock.
  Who's there?
Donahue.
  Donahue who?
Donahue want to
play hide-and-seek?

Knock-knock.
  Who's there?
Freddy.
  Freddy who?
Freddy or not,
here I come!

Knock-knock.
  Who's there?
Stu.
  Stu who?
Stu late to hide!

Knock-knock.
  Who's there?
Ron.
  Ron who?
Ron home!

Knock-knock.
  Who's there?
Emma.
  Emma who?
Emma 'fraid of the dark.

Knock-knock.
  Who's there?
Hugh.
  Hugh who?
Hugh go way!

Knock-knock.
  Who's there?
Ivan.
  Ivan who?
Ivan to haunt you.

Knock-knock.
  Who's there?
Boo.
  Boo who?
Well, you don't have to cry about it.

Knock-knock.
　Who's there?
Little old lady.
　Little old lady who?
I didn't know you could yodel.

Knock-knock.
　Who's there?
Hans.
　Hans who?
Hans up!

Knock-knock.
　Who's there?
Holden.
　Holden who?
Holden up the train.

Knock-knock.
   Who's there?
Yah.
   Yah who?
Ride 'em cowboy!

Knock-knock.
   Who's there?
Danielle.
   Danielle who?
Danielle so loud!

Knock-knock.
  Who's there?
Llama.
  Llama who?
Llama Yankee Doodle Dandy!

Knock-knock.
  Who's there?
Lionel.
  Lionel who?
Lionel roar when
he sees you!

Knock-knock.
  Who's there?
Ken.
  Ken who?
Ken I give the elephant
a peanut?

Knock-knock.
  Who's there?
Phil.
  Phil who?
Phil like giving him
another one?

Knock-knock.
  Who's there?
Thea.
  Thea who?
Thea later, alligator.

Knock-knock.
  Who's there?
Harry.
  Harry who?
Harry up and
open the door!

Knock-knock.
  Who's there?
Leif.
  Leif who?
Leif me alone.

Knock-knock.
  Who's there?
Adam.
  Adam who?
Adam my way!
I'm coming in!

Knock-knock.
  Who's there?
Omar.
  Omar who?
Omar goodness, what's that?

Knock-knock.
  Who's there?
Les.
  Les who?
Les go for a swim.

Knock-knock.
  Who's there?
Tommy.
  Tommy who?
Tommy ache!

Knock-knock.
  Who's there?
Ethan.
  Ethan who?
Ethan this a nice picnic?

Knock-knock.
  Who's there?
Barbie.
  Barbie who?
Barbie-cue chicken!

Knock-knock.
  Who's there?
Sid.
  Sid who?
Sid down in your seat.

Knock-knock.
  Who's there?
Hiawatha.
  Hiawatha who?
Hiawatha bad today.

Knock-knock.
  Who's there?
Bea.
  Bea who?
Bea-have or you stay after school!

Knock-knock.
   Who's there?
Oscar.
   Oscar who?
Oscar silly question
and you get a silly answer.

Knock-knock.
   Who's there?
Hutch.
   Hutch who?
Did you sneeze?

Knock-knock.
   Who's there?
Quiet Tina.
   Quiet Tina who?
Quiet Tina classroom!

Knock-knock.
    Who's there?
Justin.
    Justin who?
Justin time for your party.

Knock-knock.
    Who's there?
Sue.
    Sue who?
Sue-prise!

Knock-knock.
  Who's there?
Abbey.
  Abbey who?
Abbey birthday!

HAPPY BIRTHDAY

Knock-knock.
  Who's there?
Bertha.
  Bertha who?
Bertha-day cake—Yum-yum!

Knock-knock.
Who's there?
Shirley.
Shirley who?
Shirley am tired of knock-knock jokes.

Knock-knock.
Who's there?
Orange juice.
Orange juice who?
Orange juice sorry this book is over?

Knock-knock.
Who's there?
Aldo.
Aldo who?
Aldo anything to get away
from these knock-knock jokes.